# Edge

# *Edge*

Poems

Emmalee Windle

Bird Brain Publishing

Evansville, Indiana

EDGE
Copyright © 2025 by Emmalee Windle

Poems by Emmalee Windle

All rights reserved. No part of this book may be reproduced or transmitted in any form or by any means, electronic or mechanical, including photocopying, recording, or by any information storage and retrieval system, without permission in writing from the publisher.

A version of "Daffodils" previously appeared in The Meadow. "The Lakefill" previously appeared in Illinois's Best Emerging Poets. "To have and to hold" previously appeared in America's Best Emerging Poets.

Cover art by: Aaron Lane
Cover design by: Laila Schu - Regent Promotions

Bird Brain Publishing is an imprint of Bird Brain Productions.

www.birdbrainproductions.com

Windle, Emmalee
    Edge / by Emmalee Windle
    Summary: original poetry

ISBN 13: 978-1-937668-09-9
            Paperback

Printed in the United States of America

*For Alex*

# Contents

Free 3
Of the Sea 5

Heaviness 7
Rose Petals 9
Le papillon tombé (The fallen butterfly) 11
The Slug and the Bee 16
The 13th of November 17
Adela in the Cave 18
hurt: 20
Passing 21
Hearing 22
Body 23
A Weathering 25
Dream 26
Four Poems 27

Lightness 33
20,000 Feet Above 35
Daffodils 36
Journal 38
The Lakefill 39
Gum 40
Lost 41
Dream, Revisited 43
To have and to hold 44
Conversation with Myself 45
One Day 46
Light: haikus 47
Edge 48

Free Again 55

# Free

When I heard the word free
I thought about the smell of freshly waxed hardwood floors
in an ancient shoebox of an apartment
and I thought about how different that oak must look now
new feet,
new voices reverberating off its surface
and I thought about the times I skinned my knees
sliding on that floor
and I wondered if it remembers that too

I thought about the tingling feeling I used to get
when my feet slid off the pavement and
I let my legs do the pumping
shoelaces undone
lips chapped
sun painted skin

I remember how it felt to be free

# Of the Sea

There lived a girl on the edge of the sea
who knew nothing but the doom she held within.
The lull and beat of the ocean's mighty din
and a bird's song her only company.
By the window's light of moon she sits to see
the place where land ends and the rest begins.
Here she waits by the bay in sea-foamed skin
for some kind bird to sing to her sweetly:
*Look at your hands. See your veins—they jump and turn.*
*Do not look to the sea to feel the pulse of waves.*
*May you not cry from the pain of coarse salt's burn*
*nor thresh in wind or spray. If you embrace*
*the tides and drifts, I swear that you will learn*
*the ebb, the flow, the course of love—be brave.*

*Heaviness*

Spring passed my window.
Her crocuses' waking heads
Burst forth life below.

## Rose Petals

My story began in silence:
I could not breathe. Or:
I would come to breathe.
Or as my mother puts it:
it was only for a moment.

That first breath filled my belly like a balloon.

When I was four,
I wrote my name
in chalk on our
apartment building's
wall. One E with
eight horizontal
lines, some passing
beyond the wall.
A hose came later,
many rains. It did
not budge—despite
my sad scrubbing.

When I was six, it was
my mother's birthday. I
put out my finger—pointed
to a sugar rose on the edge
of the cake. It happened
fast. Or: my mother's
instinct did too. The knife
touched briefly with no pain.

Picture if you will a warm night,
a third floor walk-up, no AC.
Two twin beds: one by the fan
where souls are sucked from their bodies,
one by the wall where servants from
a time passed are buried. Or:
this is what my sister told me.
And: I slept on the carpet
between the two beds.

Do you believe in God?
At least believe most objects
in nature are symmetrical:
eyes set on the side of a fly's head,
the veins of a leaf. Such design
facilitates survival.
Some things are meant to live,

imprinted on a brick wall or a mind,
pressed between two pages of a book.

# Le papillon tombé (The fallen butterfly)

**Grand Jeté**

When we were young, the world lay just outside of reach
and on tiptoes even, only our bodies held us back from reaching far enough.
If we could only be more—
In order to empower us as young women, the elementary dance teacher gave the same
motivational speech each year, with which she ended,

> *Believe*
> *and your body*
> *will listen.*

**Chassé**

After four years of corps de ballet,

        Emma landed the role of Farfalla in Le Papillon.

*Ethereal, and diaphanous, an intangible*

        *artist imperative,* she commanded attention on opening night.

Those close enough to hear her slippers

        beat the floor sat enraptured by her urgency.

A brilliant white skirt,

        the playful pluck of strings,

legs fluttering,

        her skin lit under stage lights,

an unbroken smile—

        while they witnessed the perfect

pirouette.

## Changement

*The smile must never fade.*
*Let it be your persistent costume.*

Emma Livry knew the importance of costume when studying in France.

She refused to wear the fireproofed muslin on stage

for it was stiff and unattractive.

She shook her loose skirts about in celebration of the battle won.

    Yet we also feel

                  deep within these bodies.

I remember

    backstage feeling my shoulders

        pulse from straps

digging into fat, trying

    to strangle it away until

one popped on stage

    tired of holding me in.

Smile, my mother mouthed from her seat,

        never let it fade.

Just then I panicked
        at how tight and round my lungs
had become, at how my painted lips felt
        like wet sand and at the curious
mound of bones I had become.

On stage your body is

a thing

        a crust to wipe away

                an insistence

                        you no longer entertain.

And I will forgive it

when it begins to listen.

**Volé**

Until her death, Emma maintained

        exquisite form, that unwavering smile

            that witnesses claimed

            haunt them still. Silent as an ember,

            a shudder swam through

        her body. In a final jeté,

a gas-light caught her skirt on fire.

            Shimming like a feather,

                she leapt across the stage

                      three times before her smile extinguished.

## The Slug and the Bee

There stick these worries deep
Within my gut of slime that pass
So slowly like the heavy tick of time—
You know a bug would never pick
A slug's slow pace to keep.

*Oh slug! You do not know*
*The beauty you are blessed to see*
*By moving at the pace which nature lives.*
*The colors are a blur to me*
*On flowers that I sow.*

If I could ever do
As much as you do in a day—
Instead I'm cursed to crawl on this low ground
And see no more than shapes of gray.
I yearn to fly like you.

*This precious gift you waste!*
*If only I could rest my wings*
*And smell a flower for its natural worth—*
*Instead I'm cursed to feel the sting*
*Of a life enslaved to haste.*

Too burdened to be free
*Too busy to enjoy the bloom*
Of all that you are, I will never be—
*The swiftness of my wings, my doom,*
The heaviness in me.

# The 13th of November

A barely-there guest bedroom off the kitchen:
She waited for the sun to rise,
For cinderblock walls to crumble with light,
To see red-orange behind her eyes.

Before the dawn broke in, another light was cast—
Light of an unnatural kind.
Then hands that turned the knob, locked the door,
Sent darkness up her spine.

Familiar, pleading hands with nails
Cut past the bit;
His callused palms, in which still beat
Her heart that lived in it.

Whom she once trusted lost her in blind rage—
Hands once loved, now feared.
But morning brought her change of heart:
Mistakes to be endeared.

For which she once had faith in him
Resumed in time at dawn.
The man she had once known returned—
The cruel man was long gone.

> We live between
> The weak and might.
> Though one deemed wrong
> And one deemed right,
>
> What lives in night
> Won't die at day.
> The sins in sight
> Not kept at bay.

# Adela in the Cave

*A Sestina*

If there's a scar, there must have been a wound.
Think back: a surface hit, a hand that struck?
Examine closely: oblong splotch of gray,
Across the outer thigh, beneath the surface
Blood moves through shattered veins to bring it life.
The sky a perfect blue above the caves.

Before gray, the mark was black as a cave
And she wore skirts that hid her wound
So it would not interfere with her life.
Once crossing the street she was almost struck
By a bus but no fear came to the surface
And only for a moment her face turned gray.

The sky above the caves a perfect gray.
The sky a perfect gray above the caves.
A wetness damped the rocks' perfect surface.
She found a fallen bird that had a wound.
Think back, she told the bird, a surface struck?
*No bother, but a wound like yours ends a life.*

She, startled, left the bird to save his own life
And felt her face turn deeper shades of gray.
Her thigh began to pulse like it'd been struck
And needing rest she headed toward the caves.
The skirt when lifted did not show her wound.
Instead she saw her skin's unblemished surface.

A thing began to breathe beneath the surface,
And suddenly she realized it was life.
A burst of fire made her heart the wound.
It turned a fiery red, consumed the gray
And whispered that her pain lay in the caves.
*The reason for her pain,* the answer struck.

There must be something in here; madness struck
her. She found only darkness and rocks' surface.
But then the darkness filled her heart, a cave.
And with the scar gone, the wound became her life.
Her fingers once full of life were warped in gray
And then she realized they had caused the wound.

hurt:

       lips:
sealed with wax
of liquor then shame
you walk more quickly,
ignore the wetness, take blame

       listen:
it's cold for September
i can't complain
classes start tomorrow
it might rain

       underwear:
red
dried into a grotesque ball
pushed to the corner of your ~~mind~~ room

       finger:
hangnail
pointed at your chest
nipples thrust through lace

snow:
       in late September
reluctant
    ugly
        chaste

# Passing

It settles on you like a fine mist
Each hair on your arm bearing
Its own drop of dew

All at once
Cleanliness is key to survival

Wash
Whatever can be washed

Sew seams
In all forgotten trousers

Iron sheets
For the unused guest room

Purchase fresh flowers

Wash the dog

Make a list
Cross it out

Make sense
Out of something

Move along

# Hearing

All I remember from that 20 minutes
was the speck of white on the woman's tooth.
As I sat at the clean table,
I looked up and sticking out of her partially parted lips
was a tooth with a tiny splotch of extra-white white,
like she was whitening her teeth when the phone rang
and in answering the phone she forgot to finish that tooth.

She said thank you, then we moved on with the hearing—
her leading us by an agenda punched into a 3-ring binder, reading a script
she took a three-hour class to learn, from which she received a certificate
she brought home to show her husband so they could smile at it and be
proud that she's "giving back" and "making a difference" by expelling men
for raping women, or instead slowly destroying survivors who will spend
the next one to three years looking over their shoulders wondering if he's
following her, if he will be in one of her classes, if she can ever feel safe again.

Who wins in a world filled with loss?

# Body

Fall in love with me — feel me —
see more than my rough    edges and pores

How could I feel anything
but your eyes examining
every inch of this not-good-enough-for-you
skin?    So I turned off

the lights before you
        could and we got so faded I couldn't
see lines between you and me anymore.
For a few hours we slept,
never    touching    in    your    bed.

In the blue light of dawn — I wouldn't recognize if you
so subtly tried to press you
                                against me— attempting
to understand my body
and its unholy inability to succumb.

No— I can't know you.
I do not feel you there.

———

she slept selfishly
tucked into the covers
naked and unrefined

he loved her almost more when
she could not suck in her soft gut
or straighten her back

she snored and drooled
and he watched goosebumps sprout
in his finger's path drawn across her body
her body was soft yet strong
her body was a memory
every scar, blemish, wrinkle
the arch of her eyebrows
the imprints clothes left around her waist and breasts
little bug bites scratched into scabs
then faded into scars

he wondered how her body will respond to another man's touch
a man who knows nothing about the softness and strength
nor that the softness is her shield and the strength is her armor
he wonders if she will quiver when he holds her tight

if he will wonder why
if he will know

# A Weathering

A piece of beach glass in my pocket
Blue-green, smooth

Held up to the light, she
Is the outline of a body

The skin around the navel
Beginning to stretch

A beating heart
Who fades

The ache of a body dying
Within another

One innocent question of
*When are you due*

A wave erodes the sharp edges
Folds into softness

                                        The ache of a body dying
                                                Blue-green, smooth

                                                        A beating heart
                                                       Within another

                                    The skin around the navel
                                        Is the outline of a body

                                One innocent question of
                                                *Who fades*

                            Waves erode the sharp edges
                                      Beginning to stretch

                                    Held up to the light, she
                                        Folds into softness

# Dream

I see your face in a dream
Flooded with light
So that your mouth is a halo

Your hands
Pressed together
Signal prayer

To a god that will hurt me

# Four Poems

**Frost**

The first time I read Frost was in second grade in a book of poems, a prize I earned for selling ten magazines.
Between that and a bag of M&M's, I chose poetry and fell in love with birch trees.
The clean image of a boy swinging them as ice storms do, the solitude of his play— they gave me some comfort that there are still beautiful things in our ugly world.

**A poem**

I wrote a poem about violence—
a nonfiction assignment in creative writing class
in the high school filled
with people who pretended they
didn't know.

The air in the room was heavy
with the promise of summer
and the reminder that despite
our strong academics
we can't afford AC.

I read boldly, not allowing
my voice to shake,
and to this day
five years later
it is still the best thing I've written.

No one spoke.
Someone coughed.
My sweaty thighs
unstuck from the metal seat.
I froze—waiting for the teacher
to respond, critique the poem.
But he only looked at me and
said, quite plainly,

*I think you should go see the counselor.*

Suddenly, I was a child, who having experienced
things a child shouldn't,
is looked at with pity
or else looked away from
quickly and denied
recognition. I was small,
but not smaller than the man
sitting on his stool in dress pants
who only looked at the ground
as I walked out.

**Right and Wrong**

We all did what we thought was right,
By the fucked up definitions of right and wrong we were taught
In between times tables and the anatomy of our bodies
When we learned that this part could go here
And three times four is eleven too many times she should have to say no.
But maybe she was wrong
For thinking her body belonged to
Only her,
For choosing to say *no* when *yes*
Would have made this all easier.

**Grand Jury**

I changed my outfit six times
before I decided on a look conveying
*fragile victim,*
*confident, but most importantly honest.*
Twelve citizens sat waiting in an oval room
Someone scotch-taped a cartoon cut-out on the door
Whose caption read 'getter prosecuted.'

We laughed nervously.
We hugged, in every combination of child and parent.
Each victim entered the room,
one girl in a conservatively, well-cut dress
with her hands by her sides
after the other.

# *Lightness*

If there is one truth of which I can be certain,
it is that nothing can be seen in absolute darkness.

A little light must be let in
if anything is to be found at all.

## 20,000 Feet Above

I wake in darkness to the sound
Of a faint ding; it's nothing more
Than someone who wants coffee, tea;
A child's whimper; a man's snore.

To see the lake beneath our wings
I lift the shade. The water reflects
The depth of black that swims the sky,
Its only purpose to perplex.

The mystery of darkness fades
As we cross land, the vicious glare
Replaced by stars as they come out
And just as quickly lose their flare.

The orbs of light shine, then turn dim
And leave an imprint of their glow.
The rhythm snares me in a trance
As we begin to dip below

The lights, until we crossed one's path.
Its flash reveals it rides on wings
That cruise through the night like ours.
So unlike the stars are man's things.

## Daffodils

Of all that we were, I remember these:
santa fe in the dry heat of august
when we walked alone for a whole day
unsupervised, trading sweaty nickels
for handfuls of malachite, or virginia beach
in a bedroom with sea green walls
that looked black, eyes hovering
like marbles, the moon dipping
in and out of the still ocean.
Do you remember?
Running to the water and hiding
our breasts in the waves,
yellow flowers with wide petals,
ripping their stems, green and smooth, open,
those yellow flowers with wide petals,
running our lips over their exposed bones to get the sweetness
—some day much later
my sister would say *daffodil*
like a grownup had placed the word
on her tongue—
riding your bike blind, the skinned side
of your thigh pushing out tiny globes of blood,
the long flat stones in our yard lifted,
the dirt tilled once more, a garden
filled with cement, the skin of your stomach
blue, stretched over a blooming seed—
returning barefoot and drunk to our backyard,
blinded, searching for yellow,
wondering what would be remembered in a few years,
if I were enough in this moment to keep living.

Your daughter is in sleeping beauty sheets damp with night sweat
dreaming of tomorrow when I promised
we'd plant flowers
the kind that come in plastic cartons
already bloomed—
there is dirt beneath her thin nails
and pain she can't yet see
poised at her wrist like a knife.

# Journal

I laughed today more than I have in a while. That felt nice. It felt good to be surrounded by people who know that I am not well but that I will be one day because I have been before.

*You are so strong.*

*So many people love you.*

*I know that you will get through this.*

I slept over at a friend's so I wouldn't be alone. She fell asleep and I listened to her sleep talk for a while. She turned over on her side—I could see it in the springs above me in the bunk bed. I heard her coo and mumble incoherent sounds. She giggled and said, *I'm so excited* and I could see the way her eyes might have lit up if they had been open and the lights had been on.

I have never seen someone's eyes so clearly in the dark.

# The Lakefill

I walked to the lake on a whim in November
in between one meeting and the next—to see
why the children took off their shoes to walk along
the rocks. There must be something magical
about the slippery coldness of the stones
on bare feet, to feel grooves carved out by waves.
Barefooted children hardly ever hesitate—
eager for the next rock to compare to the last.
I sat on the green and watched them pick and choose
their rocks, paths along the coast weaving here and there.
Their heads dipped up and down beneath the slope, moving
along the wall of rocks, some sprayed by waves who dared
to venture lower, others treading near the grass—
still some sat crosslegged on the green and watched boats
bobbing up and down. There was something sad, I think,
about the pensive look they wore when they—silent—
gazed out at sea. It was as if they knew
too much between the sea and sky, that now they need
no comfort in finding where one began, nor where
the other ends; nor do they blaze a path between
the two where children so often fall and scrape knees,
or lose their glasses, or drop their candy in the sea.

# Gum

I put gum behind my ear before we started talking
and after you turned the camera on.
I thought it would make you laugh.
That's worth catching on film.
I wanted to watch that over and over again.
You smiled weakly,
glancing to the camera to make sure it was recording.
You cleared your throat, then I did mine.

I woke up the next morning with gum stuck in my hair.
It tangled itself into a big knot that had to be cut out.
My hair was short like a boy's, you always said.

You saw the sticky blue-crusted brown hair in the trash can
and collapsed to the ground, out of breath, in a fit of laughter.

# Lost

What I have lost:
trust in white men
the clarity of memory
that Indian place off the Jarvis stop

You took me there on a date
ten months before

After the hearing,
after you were expelled and
shipped back to Florida,
a friend of mine got in some trouble
for what he said was

*all her fault*

I held his hand
coached his apology speech
cried when he was expelled and
shipped back to Iowa

I saw a picture of him six months later
thumbs-up in a new dorm room
at a state college where no one knew
anything but that charming smile

Pain leaves the body
with nothing but its memory

Yet memories can be deceiving
you may have thought (you said no)
but you were wrong

Five years later
I wonder at the permeability
of the past

For anyone can dip a hand
into a memory and rearrange it

# Dream, Revisited

My mother and I walked up
the ramp of the parking garage
with the easy gait of those
who have nowhere in particular
to be. A soft, timeless
meandering. Maybe we had
forgotten where we parked
the car. Or maybe we were
trying to extend the kinetic
energy between two people
who have just watched a play
together but can't yet wrap
their minds around it.
We walked in silence
until we heard the low voices of
men around the next bend.
Then the hearty sound of a man's
laugh with the slightest tinge
of violence in it.
Our pace did not change
but was now imbued with a sense
of urgent hesitation.
I pulled a gun from my bag
and shot it in the air—as a warning.
My mother grabbed her chest,
exclaimed, *they shot me.*
But I knew that I was killing her.

## To have and to hold

You started with the words *they say marriage is through good times and*—
I cut you off with the snap of a towel around my body

And now I write out our story like currency—
words of silver dollars that give this poem value

And now my hands smell like the garlic
I pressed to rid my mouth the taste of you

# Conversation with Myself

*I'm so desolate, I've begun to crave nonexistence,*
she gently said to me in the intimacy of her linen closet.
I wrapped a string around my wrist to a light bulb that wasn't there.
Her breath was heavy, her lips cracked and wet
as she leaned closer and buried her troubles
in the hollow of my neck. Suddenly
the bulb was there, lit between her thumb and index.
*I'm losing you.*
I reveled in the sound of anguish,
reverberating off her body and sinking
into the coats—every syllable dripped in sentiment.
*I can feel it in the weariness that grips the corners of your lips.*
*Where are you?*
Suddenly the bulb was gone.
The string hung purposeless,
ashamed of its vulnerability.
My mind paced, seeking a way to fix her.
*It is not where; it's who.*
*I am you.*
She opened the door that separated us from the rest of the world
and left me.

# One Day

*A Villanelle*

One day, I will walk on water,
let the folks see me stepping across the pain.

"Miracle," Kwame Dawes

One day I will walk on water.
See me break from shore and cross the bay
and watch how my feet no longer falter

but carry me deep into poetic wander
to seek the depths of what my voice can say.
One day I will walk on water

and my mother will hear her daughter,
tumbling from her lap, whisper *let me stray.*
Watch how my feet no longer falter

at the failure fated by my father
who promised me that poets may
never one day walk on water.

So I lay my words on a page like an altar
and pouring out my soul, I pray
to one day see my feet not falter,

to find truth in pain, the core unaltered.
See me break from shore, the lure to stay,
and watch how my feet no longer falter.
One day, I will walk on water.

# Light:

*haikus*

Out of darkness, I
emerge. Warrior of light,
taste my silence break.

Triumphant, my eyes
see all that once was not mine—
feet, hands, unfettered.

Feel the force of one
who once thrashed against the hold
of stronger hands, nails—

Find not hate for those
who ripped clothes off her body,
or disappointment,

Not even vengeance
to right the wrong, the stale fault
of many—but love.

This body is soft.
Broken—yes. Hurt—yes. And strong
and wise. Yes, wisdom

it carries to speak,
rebuild what was once destroyed
with the pain of love.

That of a mother,
laboring to death for life.
Hold on hope, she says.

That of my sisters,
their voices drowning sorrow
in triumphant song.

We are more than hurt
parts of a body attacked.
Feel our silence break.

# Edge

Before I left, I stored the Midwest landscape in my memory
like soft dollars in a back pocket put through the wash:
a land flat for miles, white as hurt; a ripped awning waves;

signs handwritten on bits of 99c poster board—the comatose
flash of casinos off the highway, a parking lot under the glow
of wings buzzing blindly into lights—*come in; it's warm here.*

That winter I spent in Nice, the weather turned warm and
the air heavy with brine. One night the tram jolted to a stop.
It kept still for a few minutes while strangers exchanged eyes

that wandered for a bit of human interaction. There was a man
in a button-down with moon-white, pearl buttons and I imagined
his veins were interstates sprawled over the bruises of a flat land

passed through. There was a woman
in spaghetti straps with tattoos contracting on
her soft sides. The night was wonder.

The night was a body of petals and these were my hands
catching them. Boarding the train, I had knocked hard
against the ungiving thrust of the turnstile too soon, and felt

the rush of blood to the surface where I'd look when I got to the hostel.
I'd peel off jeans to find no bruise to show— only the memory
of metal against flesh and the blank look of I'm-not-looking-at-you.

At night, walking alone to catch people in the open-aired bistros
eat ice cream and sip café au lait, I failed to notice the way the waves
folded into the beach. They grazed the shore as if they too were caught

in the spell of a bourgeois sea town that felt it could, when a woman
catches the smell of salt left by her hair on a pillow, be recalled
again and again as some distant memory. The woman seated across

from me on the tram caught my glance. She wore the unabashed grin
of tilling the other. I, arrested in her gaze, believed
that my anonymity had dissolved, that my story was already repeating

in her memory. We now know that when an event is
remembered, we recall the memory of the first time we recalled it.
The pure memory of it is lost in the endless archives of our minds

where weaves of biases and misinterpretations tangle
the strands of what had been. Can we believe that
whatever happens, this is?

Before Nice, an organic farm farther north:
Snow, seventeen inches over night.
The worst winter Bargème had seen in decades.

Once a week we Skyped—
me on the farm's one desktop computer
you amidst a hungover afternoon stench in Ohio

as I tell all: the rooster that died
splinters from carrying wood
my baby toe, turned blue from frostbite.

Weekly, I watched our connection unravel like
the dropped stitches
in the scarf I taught myself how to knit.

For you
I knit a full set— scarf, hat, gloves—
while my toes froze in too-big boots and Hanes Socks for Ladies.

To France, I brought only the essentials: books (never read),
cigarettes, and my grandparent's wedding album. At night,
unable to sleep, I reveled in the simplicity of

Clara Stagg and Charles Remley's Midwest marriage:
*I wore this brown tea-length dress, very simple. That's what we did
in the 50s, afternoon weddings were quite modest. We served*

*cake n' punch, nothing else. 30 or so people came.* My mother's voice echoes
the grandmother I never met. *Cake n' punch.* And I feel the grittiness
of sugar on my teeth.

My mother tells me that they never spent a night apart,
through decades of marriage. I tell her I think Plath said it best, that the world
is splitting open at my feet like a ripe, juicy watermelon, that its sweet nectar

runs down my arms in comforting rivers of pinkness. I wake
in the morning to the sound of a rooster, make yogurt from real cream,
shower once a week. They don't use napkins at dinner, and talk so fast

I cannot understand a word. When do I laugh? Shake my head?
Say 'non, merci' or 'oui merci?' I cling to the words in your emails.
How much I appreciate the familiarity of English, your voice.

I came to the foothills to write, am rendering nothing
worth the mention. My story, or rather the need to tell it,
feels stale. I thought myself brave yet I am strangely small here.

In Florence, you participate in *aperitif* hour. You feel adult-like,
hot from wine. Your friends are drunk; their friends speak
in accents that make you weak, aroused by their foreignness.

You might be manic.
Words tumble out after three months of self-induced silence.
Soon, someone is whispering in your ear,
*you're making this so easy.*

I want what they had.
    *Who?*

You can't give it to me.
    *Give what?*

There's a heaviness between us.
    *My body is the heaviness;*

feel it pull you and warp you in memory. You are
the bruise on the inside of my thigh not purple
or bloodied like a galaxy but flesh-colored, invisible.

The spaghetti strap woman's smile lingers.
She too knows about the heaviness.
My grandmother's hands are her hands.

Her memory is full of soft dollars.
Her teeth are gritty with the sugar
of too much cake.

She too has woken to the Duomo's
resounding bells and missed
the familiarity of touch.

           I am a body and hers,
   a cupped hand
that catches mine.

## Free Again

A pebble skips three times over water.
Each time it asks
*Are you alright?*
*What happened?*
*How can I help?*
I will listen
To the soft vibrations of your ripples
Folding out onto the lake.

A pebble skips three times over water.
Each time it tells you
*All is well.*
*I am here.*
*Be still.*
I will stand on the edge
Of your water
And feel your tiny waves
Folding out onto the lake.

# Notes

"Rose Petals" was inspired by Louise Glück's "Faithful and Virtuous Night."

A version of "Daffodils" previously appeared in *The Meadow*.

"The Lakefill" previously appeared in *Illinois's Best Emerging Poets*.

"To have and to hold" previously appeared in *America's Best Emerging Poets*.

www.ingramcontent.com/pod-product-compliance
Lightning Source LLC
LaVergne TN
LVHW041346080426
835512LV00006B/647